THE

# VALLEY OF ACHOR A DOOR OF HOPE;

OR, THE

# GRAND ISSUES OF THE WAR.

## A DISCOURSE,

DELIVERED ON

THANKSGIVING DAY, NOV. 26, 1863.

BY

HENRY CLAY FISH, D.D.,

PASTOR OF FIRST BAPTIST CHURCH, NEWARK, N. J.

New-York:

SHELDON & CO., 335 BROADWAY.

1863.

# THE VALLEY OF ACHOR A DOOR OF HOPE;

OR, THE

# GRAND ISSUES OF THE WAR.

## A DISCOURSE,

DELIVERED ON

THANKSGIVING DAY, NOV. 26, 1863.

BY

HENRY CLAY FISH, D.D.,

PASTOR OF FIRST BAPTIST CHURCH, NEWARK, N. J.

New-York:

SHELDON & CO., 335 BROADWAY.

1863.

Note.—This discourse was repeated Sabbath evening, November 29th, in the presence of an audience numbering over two thousand persons, when a copy was requested for publication.

# DISCOURSE.

HOSEA 2: 15.

"AND I will give her the valley of Achor for a door of hope."

THE valley of Achor was some ten miles north of Jerusalem, and not far from Bethel, the place of Jacob's vision. It was called *Achor* from the word *Achan* or *Achar*, which was applied to it from an incident in the travels of the Israelites, recorded in the seventh of Joshua. Here it was that Achan sinned in taking the Babylonish garment, and the shekels of silver and the wedge of gold among the spoils of the enemy, which were denominated accursed things—and for this impiety he was stoned with stones, and then burnt to ashes, after which the wrath of God was appeased. This valley was called Achar or Achor, from the name of this man, Achan. And the word Achan itself means *troubler*, so that the valley was known for many generations, as *the valley of trouble.* Hence the term came to be used to describe *any* position of special trial or trouble. He who was in some terrible extremity, was spoken of as being *in the valley of Achor.*

And so it was that seven hundred years later than the occurrence here referred to, we hear the prophet Hosea, in our text, using this same figurative expression. He is announcing God's reconciliation with his erring people, and the mercies which he would surely bestow, *after* the sore discipline for their sins. "I will speak comfortably unto her, and I will give her vineyards from thence, and *the valley of Achor for a door of hope,* and she shall sing there as in the days of her youth, and as in the day when she came up out of the land of Egypt."

The idea of the prophet is this: Israel found deliverance of old, in that very valley of trouble. There the fierce anger of God was turned away, and his smiles were vouchsafed, and her songs of rejoicing were heard. And now am I about to repeat the deliverance. You are brought low, but your very place of trouble, your *valley of Achor*, shall be a *door of hope.* "And I will give her the valley of Achor for a door of hope, and she shall *sing* there, as in the days of her youth."

And herein is seen a law of the divine economy. It seems a principle from which God does not often deviate, that the door of hope should be in the valley of Achor:—that seasons of trouble should precede the richest experience of his goodness.

I. Proceed with me while I endeavor, first, TO ESTABLISH AND ILLUSTRATE THIS PRINCIPLE.

And to begin; do we not gather an intimation of such a divine plan in the work of *creation?* In its original state, our earth was without form and void, and *darkness* was upon the face of the deep. And the record of its reconstruction, again and again repeated, runs thus: "and the evening and the morning were the (particular) day." Historically, the evening, the *night*, came first. The day was composed of darkness and light, but the *darkness preceded* the light. Who shall say that there was not, in this natural phenomenon, a hint of the fact under consideration? And the most extended and minute examination will show how widely and profoundly this fact applies to the *moral world.*

You may divide the past centuries into epochs, and write concerning them as of the original epochs of creation, "and the evening and the morning were the (new) day." They will be seen to be made up of periods of darkness and of light—the darkness, however, always going before and preparing for the light. The history of man really begins in his apostasy. It was but a gleam of sunshine that fell on his forehead in Paradise, when he was enveloped in the darkness and blindness of sin, *the emerging from which* really makes his history. At this low point, after the fall, in the gulf of deep distress, the social life of man began to improve, and it has been making steady advances ever since. It was in this *valley of trouble* that the coming Messiah was first revealed. And what a *door of hope* was there opened in those words, "The seed of the woman shall bruise the serpent's head." From that time forward, whenever darkness came on, it was but the beginning of a new day, and each new day (like those in Genesis) was in advance of the day that preceded it. The night was the period of gestation, of preparation. Forms of civilization decayed, in long succession, but each worn-out form carried in its bosom elements which gave birth to a new and more perfect form. Great and mighty institutions gave way to either time, or revolution, or foreign invasion, but the germs of a new life were always existing in each decaying institution, and the period of decline for one people or age was a period of purifying process or preparation for that age or people that should succeed it.

Thus Central India, the earliest of the historical na tions, began in obscurity, reached a high position, then declined. But even this our age is enriched by its old

Sanscrit tongue and many elements of its philosophy. Egypt emerged from darkness into light, and then its sun set; but not until it had thrust forward into the Judaic and other nations its real acquisitions, there to receive a higher development. The same may be said of Assyria, and each of the old Eastern nations. So of Greece and Rome in the West. From small beginnings, and through innumerable difficulties, they forced their way up to greatness; but though their philosophy and theology had in them the seeds of death, and so decayed, yet how greatly, through their laws, and literature, and arts, have they contributed to prepare the world for its present condition.

In how low a vale of trouble, too, did the Israelitish nation begin its career—in the bondage of Egypt and in the discipline of the wilderness. And though it vanished away, yet it was but to give room to the *Christian* civilization that was to follow. I might also point you to the old ancestral peoples of Europe, from whom we and the several now powerful nations have sprung, and show how they struggled into being, and how, too, their death was our life. Read d'Aubigné's last work and Alison's Europe, and behold the upturning of the nations that ended in the great Reformation. Follow the graphic pen of Macaulay, and behold the series of English revolutions, from the Long Parliament to the settlement of William and Mary on the throne, and see how the Bill of Rights and other reforms were born. Ireland was in rebellion; Scotland in rebellion; powerful continental combinations were counter-working the liberties of England; the finances were in a deplorable condition; the court and army were demoralized; vindictive parties were plotting the ruin of both church and state; and yet, out of these ruinous complications arose British power in all its subsequent magnificence.

And how true this was of the immediate founders of this republic, we all well know. They too passed through the Red Sea of suffering and the desert of trial, and *then*, and not before, came into their Canaan. And so all along the track of time have the *valleys of Achor* been turned into *doors of hope.* There is not a nation now advanced in the world's civilization, that has not won its place by long years of severe and perhaps terrific effort.

And the same is true of the *religious* progress of the world. The wickedness of the antediluvians became great, and they were cut off; but the flood became a door of hope — a God-fearing people springing up in the land. The cities of the plain rioted in sensuality, and they were burned up; but their destruction arrested the general decay. The wars and tumults of Samuel's and David's time ushered in the meridian splendor of Solomon's reign. The rending of Israel into two parts hastened the extermination of idolatry. How terrible the night in which the old dispensation closed! — no voice of prophet breaking its gloom for four hundred years, and but here and there *one* "waiting for the consolation of Israel." Upon *that* night arose the Star of Bethlehem! What an Achor, what a place of trouble, the land of Judea then! What a door of hope, in David's Son, was there opened to a world! And a little later, what do we see? The heaviest troubles gathering upon the infant Church. Peter denies his Lord. Judas betrays him. The disciples are bewildered, and scattered as sheep without a shepherd; for the sword has smitten that Shepherd, and he is now dead, and *buried!* What blackness of darkness! Not a streak of day! But, again, what do we see? The clayey seals of the tomb cracking and crumbling asunder. The stone receding. The sleeper awaking. The news spreading. The enemies confounded. The Messiahship admitted. The Saviour going up in clouds. The Holy Spirit coming down in torrents of power. Banners of the Cross unfurled. The nations permeated with the Gospel. Oh! *what* an *Achor*, the place of crucifixion! Oh! *what* a *door of hope!* Remember, too, how Zion languished in the middle ages, and how this depression was succeeded by the glorious Reformation.

Observe in all this, how true it is that seasons of trouble usually precede and prepare the way for the richest experience of God's goodness; not because these depressions in *themselves* originate the better state, (for this they could not do,) but because God overrules evils, and out of them educes good; and because *vigor* is the child only of *struggle*.

We consider this law, then, a clearly established one.

"Not first the bright, and after that the dark;
But first the dark, and after that the bright;
First the thick cloud, and then the rainbow's arc;
First the dark grave, and then the resurrection light.

"'Tis first the night—stern night of storm and war,
Long night of heavy clouds and vailed skies;
*Then* the fair sparkle of the morning Star,
That bids the saint awake and day arise."

II. I proceed now to APPLY THIS LAW TO OUR PRESENT NATIONAL CONDITION.

I ask you to observe, for our instruction and encouragement, that the Valley of Achor where we now are, is becoming to us a door of hope. I shall speak of only two particulars.

1. In this vale of difficulty and sorrow, *we are recovering our lost manhood.*

Mr. Beecher said, with truth, in one of those addresses of his in England, which have at the same time reflected honor upon himself and so benefited our country's cause as to lay us under a lasting debt of gratitude, that the most valuable possession of a people was its manhood. We might lose our harvests, our houses, almost any possession, and recover them; but our manliness gone, all was gone. The first and highest quality of true manhood is more easily appreciated than defined. It is that something which the old Romans called VIR, (whence our *virtue.*) The Apostle Peter refers to it as one of the Christian graces: "Add to your faith virtue"—not (as here meant) that outward conformity to God's law which makes an upright life; but rather manly vigor, a courageous tone of mind—manliness, true manhood. We might call it force of character, boldness, firmness in whatever duty requires. Isaac Taylor paraphrases it as "manly energy, or the constancy and courage of manly vigor." Dr. Schauffler, speaking of the Crimean campaign, says the soldiers held on and took Sevastopol not by science, but by *pluck;* and that what we needed to take the strongholds of heathenism was *Christian pluck.* General Havelock spoke of *British pluck.* Sir Walter Scott speaks of a "want of *pluck*" as a sad defect in a man. The same idea is in the triplet:

> "Could'st thou not watch one hour? then sleep enough,
> That sleep may hasten manhood, and sustain
> The faint, pale spirit with some *muscular stuff.*"

This "*manhood,*" or "*muscular stuff,*" or "pluck," is the virtue commended by Peter, and the precise quality to which I refer. It is a fine trait, which every one admires. We see it in Daniel, and the three worthies, whose answer to threats was: "We are not careful to answer thee, O King, in this matter." And in Paul and Silas, who would sooner listen to the clanking of their own chains than to the voice of seduction. And in the Huguenots and Scotch Covenanters, whose heroic daring in the right flashes out like brilliant orbs in extended darkness. And in Savonarola, the Italian monk, who, when excommunicated by the Pope for his fidelity, went to the stake, saying: "From the Pope I appeal to the *heavenly* Pope, Christ Jesus." And in Luther, who, before the Court of the German empire, looked up calmly when his sentence was read, and replied: "Then God be my helper; for I can retract nothing." In such cases there was *lofty courage from principle.* There was a supreme *regard for the right*, and a *determination to pursue it* at all hazards.

Now certainly this is the first and chief ingredient in true manhood. Indeed, without it men are not men. Without it, a nation is no nation. Sir William Jones's answer to the question, "What constitutes a state?" hits the case exactly:

"Not high-raised battlement or labored mound;
Thick wall or moated gate;
Not cities proud with spires and turrets crowned;
Not bays and broad-armed ports,
Where, laughing at the storm, rich navies ride;
Not starred and spangled courts,
Where low-browed baseness wafts perfume to pride.
No: *men, high-minded* men,
With powers as far above dull brutes endued
In forest, brake, or den,
As beasts excel cold rocks and brambles rude;
Men who their duties know,
But know their rights, and knowing, *dare maintain*;
Prevent the long-aimed blow,
And crush the tyrant while they rend the chain:
*These* constitute a state."

This trait especially the people of these States were fast losing. It was far gone. Like an individual, a nation has a perception which it may sophisticate, a conscience which it may suppress, a self-respect which it may forfeit, a soul, a life, which it may lose. And it may pass out insensibly, oozing away imperceptibly. So it was with us. We had almost reached the point where we were ready to sell our birthright for a mess of pottage. We were engrossed in material pursuits. What we were after was to suck fatness out of our broad, deep soil, and our mechanic arts, and our world-wide commerce, and our positions of trust and honor, open to all, high or low, learned or illiterate, good or bad.

The sacrifice of conscience and other high qualities, to gain these ends, we were not slow to make A gigantic power had reared itself upon the gains of unrighteousness, and was holding out in one hand gold and in the other office; and if these were to be permanently proffered and enjoyed, there must be homage, acquiescence.

Mythology tells us that in the ancient days of Rome a chasm opened in the midst of the city, and streets were broken up, palaces toppled in the yawning gulf, and dwellings were swallowed in the ruin. The sages met and in council decided that by the offering of the most valuable things they possessed, the angry gods would be appeased and Rome be saved. So "the people assembled, patrician and plebeian, nobleman and slave, bringing all precious jewels, rich garments, and whatever was most rare and costly, and cast them into the chasm; but still it opened insatiate, and the fissures spread, and destruction seemed sure. But while still the terror-stricken multitude thronged the streets, there came to them, armed as one who goes to battle, riding as one who rides to victory, the noblest of their patrician sons, the very flower of their chivalry, and as the wondering crowd swayed and parted to make way, he exclaimed: '*Manhood* is the most valuable thing Rome possesses!' For an instant horse and rider hang in mid air, then down—crashing—are lost, and the dreadful abyss closes up." And so would *this* false god be appeased with nothing short of *Manhood!*

And the "sages" advised the offering, and were quick to give the example. Hordes of politicians might be seen marked and ticketed, "*For sale to the highest bidder.*" Merchants and mechanics could not safely have opinions of their own, lest their customers should be offended, so they parted with them. Greed and selfishness were fast gaining ascendency over all ranks and classes. Love of freedom, love of country, the fear of God, honor, integrity, honesty, benevolence, the public good—these were overborne and forgotten in the mad pursuit of money or popularity. Gain dragged even the ark of God in its ox-cart, and made the very minisisters of the sanctuary the echoes of them that hired them. And so the iron car of our national Juggernaut rolled on, over the Bible, the Sabbath, the sanctuary, and eternal right and mercy and justice, until there was danger of such a general demoralization of the soul of the nation, as should change us from the God-fearing, conscience-animated, sound-hearted people that our fathers were, into a race of moral pigmies, whose creed should be, "Let us eat and drink, for to-morrow we die."

Already from this cause had we become the scorn of the civilized world. "They are rotten before they are ripe," said a British reviewer of us, more in sorrow than in anger. And the good De Gasparin, who has so ably written in our behalf, admits that for many years we "had been rapidly degenerating in the whole tone of our national life."

It is alarming to think how far this had gone. Our

halls of legislation were the arena of braggarts and bullies and political hucksters and selfish squabbles, where great measures were scarcely discussed, and great minds felt themselves degraded. Not a few were tired even of our form of government, and began to think that Republicanism was a failure. A high authority declares that he knew there were thousands, if not millions, who would have welcomed an Emperor of France or of Russia, if they could have been assured of stability in their business matters; and I suppose it to be a fact that at the close of Mr. Buchanan's administration, the mind of the North was subsiding into the conviction that it was not worth while to try to interpose any check to the ruinous course of events. Even in Boston were men heard to say, "No coercion, no coercion;" and it now seems clear that had the South managed their cause wisely, they would either have gained a recognition or revolutionized the country.

So far had our manhood departed! How had the gold become dim, and the fine gold changed!

But just here, in this our valley of Achor, was opened a "door of hope." In the providence of God things took such shape that we were shut up to civilized warfare. The issue was clear and simple. Our enemies declared that the country must consent to be severed in twain, (to bleed to death,) or the government must be overthrown and destroyed. The stars and stripes are shot from the flag-staff of a national fort, and the flag of rebellion flaunts defiance in its stead. The live spot that was left in the Northern heart, throbs. With the thunder of guns and the gleam of bayonets the inward fire kindles; and first in one section, then in another, and then in another, is heard the cry: "In the name of our God we will set up our banners!"

"Lay down the axe; fling by the spade;
Leave in its track the toiling plough;
The rifle and the bayonet blade
For arms like yours were fitter now;
And let the hands that ply the pen
Quit the light task, and learn to wield
The horseman's crooked brand, and rein
The charger on the battle-field.

"Our country calls; away! away!
To where the blood-stream blots the green.
Strike to defend the gentlest sway
That Time in all its course has seen.
See, from a thousand coverts—see!
Spring the armed foes that haunt her track!
They rush to smite her down, and we
*Must* beat the banded traitors back!"

The effect was electric. War is a great educator. Napoleon rightly said: "There are always ideas at the point of the bayonet." Florence Nightingale wrote to one of the British volunteer brigades: "One who has seen more than any man what a horrible thing war is, yet feels, more than any man, that the military spirit in a good cause—that of one's country—is the finest leaven which exists for the national spirit." And she speaks of it as *retempering* a nation. There are multitudes who could never be rallied to the support of a government or any great cause, upon a question of right, who will yet be stirred by the bugle-blast of war; and once aroused they go on to a higher manhood. The power to do and to suffer is developed in great national struggles. Men learn the lessons of obedience to the "powers that be," and the subordinance of personal advantage to the public good; they learn to value those rights and privileges for which they have poured out blood and treasure; they learn to deny themselves, and to work for objects beyond them.

selves. Patriotism is thereby inflamed and becomes henceforth an inspiration; for some must give themselves to the country's service, some their sons and husbands, brothers and fathers; some their property, some their time, and all their prayers.

No trifling thing, indeed, is it, that these stirring events are instilling such qualities into this people, and kindling in their bosoms the same noble fires that burned in their honored sires. The influence is already seen, and will be more and more apparent. Already our merchants, by their sacrifices, have raised their lives to a higher level of dignity; already the most frivolous of our young women have gained a deeper and nobler sense of their own worth by their voluntary labors for the soldiers: and altogether we are certainly a more manly people than we were three years ago. We are more patriotic. That flag of country, how much dearer! It is more to us now than a piece of striped and dotted bunting—a great deal more! It brings tears to the eyes to look upon it! Who *feels* not, too, that he is more of a man, and is not prouder to be called an *American?* We stand more erect! We have done with base obsequiousness! We have more faith, too, and more patience, and a sterner sense of right. We are more thoughtful and intelligent. The national mind is jostled and set a-going. How many persons take a daily or semi-weekly paper now that took none before, and study the map, and keep posted as to all that passes, and talk learnedly about men and measures and places a thousand miles away, and read long addresses and fine-spun diplomatic letters, and have even a sharp eye to see what England, and France, and Russia are doing! Besides, we are much less trammelled by *party*. And we have done with compromises, and abominate all half measures, and have made up our minds to risk life, property, *any thing* that is called for, and to see the *end* of this struggle, and to show to the world that "there is sap in the old tree yet,"—that the pilgrim stock has not wholly degenerated:—and to prove that we *do* prize courage and manliness and unblenching devotion to country, and humanity, and God, higher than material prosperity or an inglorious peace; and that we *do* know what it is to act from a calm and resolute sense of duty, the prime essential of manhood.

Is not this war, then, an educator? Is it not the alembic from which we are emerging with nobler energies and a higher life? I, for one, can not doubt it. I believe that the returning soldiers will have gained valuable experience, and will make better men and better Christians. I verily believe, (and for this I bless God every day,) that the people generally are passing through that transformation which Tennyson describes in the career of one of his individuals. We shall

> —"wake to the higher aims,
> Of a land that has lost for a little her lust of gold
> And love of a peace that was full of wrongs and shames—
> Horrible, hateful, monstrous, not to be told.
> Though many a light shall darken, and many shall weep
> For those that are crushed in the crash of jarring claims,
> Yet God's just doom shall be wreaked on a giant liar;
> And many a darkness into the light shall leap
> And shine in the sudden making of splendid names,
> And noble thought be freer under the sun,
> And the heart of the people beat with one desire."

2. In the valley of Achor *we are recovering the jewel of the world's Freedom.*

He who supposes this war is to affect only this country, has very narrow views of things. It is for all time and for the whole race. The Rappahannock is the river of the earth. Chattanooga is the fighting ground of the world. Battles here are the world's battles. We are contending for ideas which are essential to liberty anywhere; and there is not an oppressed being on the globe—oppressed by *any* species of usurpation—that has not an interest in this conflict. We are watched of kings and peasants. Our free institutions—free schools, cheap government, voluntary religion, open ballot-box,—were before shaking the monarchies of the old world, and all eyes are now turned hither to see whether we succeed or fail, as involving their own destiny:—the king his crown, the peasant his liberty.

Is there a spot on the globe where men are practically free and equal, where they *fully* enjoy their heaven-given rights, except in this country? England comes nearest to it; but in Great Britain the people are rather for the government than the government for the people. Royalty, aristocracy, nobility, hereditary wealth and position—these things are of great moment there; and unless one can lay claim to some of them, he stands a poor chance to rise. The English poor, the laboring classes, have few rights and privileges; they are little above the serfs of Russia. It is considered that they are *born* to this condition, and the laws of the realm place the power of government principally in the hands of the land-owners and property-holders, and nobly descended. In *this* country we hold that every man is nobly born; that liberty in the highest sense is his birthright; that the poorest is entitled to just the same protection, just the same advantages of all kinds, as the wealthiest. There are here no *privileged classes.* One class is of right, in every possible respect, just as "*privileged*" as another. These are fundamental ideas in the structure of this government.

Now the oppressed of every realm *know* these are our peculiar ideas, and they yearn for their universality. They hope for the good time when they will be adopted in their own countries, and many of them would gladly come here to have the advantage of them. And we have these ideas—mark it—as a *sacred trust from God.* We have no right to throw them away, nor to let them be wrested from us. We are the *stewards* of these gifts for *earth's millions*, the guardians and almoners of their rights, (now denied them to a greater or less extent,) and sacredly bound to bring them to their possession, as far as we may. Were we to allow them to be wrested from us, we were the most faithless of mortals; and the down-trodden, whose voice we can not hear, would cry out in Heaven's ear against us!

FREEDOM, then, in its highest sense, and widest sense, is at stake in this contest. Freedom for the *enslaved blacks* on our own soil is *one* of the things involved, and a very important one. Long enough has it been denied, and all true hearts rejoice that it is being granted to them, and also that by their splendid military bearings, and their self-help in various ways, they are at once justifying their claim to manhood and acquiring that discipline, and knowledge, and experience which will aid them greatly when thrown at length upon their own resources. Freedom for the "*poor whites*" of the South is another thing involved, and a very important one. Their condition has been miserable indeed—in some respects more pitiable than that of the slaves. The planters, the slave-owners, the haughty monarchs of the soil, have domineered over them, and despised them, and well-nigh ground humanity out of them. *They* are interested in the issue of the struggle. And then freedom for *our brethren far away* (as I have said,) is another thing involved. For if we fail here, and above us darkness gathers, what star of hope remains in the whole horizon?

I said rightly, then, that in this struggle we stand for the world, we represent the world. *For the world freedom lives or dies here and now!*

Now mark this. We came near losing this priceless boon, and therefore I speak of *recovering* it. The slave power was fearfully encroaching upon our boasted liberty. Free speech was denied in one half of our territory—just as fully so as in any part of the globe—and was imperilled in the other half; and the press was in the same condition. The "higher law" was scoffed at in the United States Senate, and by the press, and even in the pulpit; and for the sake of union the infamous "Fugitive Slave" Bill was enacted, which forbade any one from practising the Christian duty of giving food and raiment and shelter to the fleeing bondman. The Supreme Court, too, had ruled the negro had no rights; and it was about to be decreed that slaves could be held in *any State, temporarily*, (while passing through it,) which was virtually conceding every thing; for if held by law one day, why not one month, or one year? Indeed, it was the boast of the Southern oligarchs that they would yet call the roll of their slaves under the shadow of Bunker Hill.

This was our condition. The commerce, the patriotism, the politics, the trade, the government, the judiciary, and the very religion of the land were infected with the spreading corruption:—yea, were under the domination of this organized iniquity. We were like Laocoön in the Vatican at Rome: 'A noble man; on either side a lovely son; but all, father and sons, grasped in the coils of a many times enfolding serpent, whose tightening hold not their utmost strength can resist, and with agonized face Laocoön looking up, as if his anguish said: 'Only the gods can save me, whose hate I have offended.'' Image of ourselves! the central Head with its clustering States, beautiful to behold, but twining around the whole the folds of the gigantic serpent, Slavery.

Dark days were those to the friends of freedom and justice! Some of us remember how we came together at the call of *another* President for formal thanksgiving, but could not tell whether our hallelujahs were looked upon by God as gratulations over a growing youth, or as funeral wails over smitten and departed glories!

But God's ways are not man's ways. We recovered the almost lost jewel of freedom in a way we never dreamed of; and might henceforth hold it with a firmer grasp and exalt it to a higher position. Wonderfully apt as illustrative of its fate are the lines of Trench:

> "A dew-drop, falling on the ocean wave,
> Exclaimed in fear—'I perish in this grave;'
> But, in a shell received, that drop of dew,
> Unto a pearl of marvellous beauty grew;
> And, happy now, the grace did magnify
> Which thrust it forth—as it had feared—to die;
> Until again, 'I perish quite,' it said,
> Torn by rude diver from its ocean bed;
> O unbelieving!—so it came to gleam,
> Chief jewel in a monarch's diadem!"

The rebellion fairly uncovered the institution which gave it birth, and made it vulnerable to Liberty's deadliest blows. Before, it was safe under local law and Federal protection. The slave-dealers were intrenched behind the bulwark of the Constitution; but now, by their own acts, it became constitutional to attack their system; nay, since it was the right arm of their power, it was impossible to maintain the integrity of that very Constitution, except by striking with all the nation's might at that institution itself. It became a military necessity to kill the monster in order to save the life of the victim. And the work of death to the former and deliverance to the latter is being rapidly done. Some few complain and demur, but still, as some one says:

> "The mower moves on, though the adder may writhe,
> And the copper-head curl round the blade of the scythe."

And every day are men of whatever political antecedents and former beliefs, coming to the resolute conviction, that there shall be no more dodging real issues, no more postponing and rolling over upon our children questions that are vital to liberty; but that slavery must be *crushed*, so as to make a clean sweep of the cause of disturbance. Said a large slave-owner from Louisiana, on a recent visit to New-York: "I speak for myself, and for the majority of loyal slaveholders in my State, when I say I want no more of slavery. It isn't profitable, and it keeps up a quarrel. I had rather that every inch of territory were trodden over by the bloody hoof of war, than that one slave should be left when it is ended." This is fast becoming the sentiment of all true patriots. The stern operator is at work. Away with all political nostrums to ease the patient! The cancer *must and shall be cut out!* This continent shall be dedicated to liberty. Our loins are girded; our hearts are fixed; our swords are drawn, and we will rest with nothing short of the freeing, by direct or indirect means, in the midst of the fiery struggle, or as close upon it, of every slave in our whole domain! And we have full faith in its accomplishment; and this because of the righteous and mighty God above us, and the underlying principle in this "irrepressible conflict."

"Can ye burn a truth in the martyr-fire?
Can ye chain a thought in a dungeon dire?—
Or stay the soul as it soars away,
In its glorious flight from its mouldering clay?
The truth that liveth, the thoughts that go,
The spirit ascending, all answer—*No.*"

And there are *truths*, there are *thoughts* in this struggle—and so it will succeed.

Happy day of the Nation's renovation! O fellow-workers, I congratulate you upon its coming in our time! I see it! I see it! The war successfully ended; the bondman everywhere a freeman; the degraded white man everywhere educated and ennobled; the diverse elements in the national composition fused and welded inseparably together; local jealousies and animosities at an end; treason and traitors expelled from the country; the heresy of state sovereignty and secession killed; loyalty and patriotism a life in the heart's core of every inhabitant; the extremities of the country drawn into a closer relationship; its physical resources developed; a school-house and church in every district; the people taking the highest type of civilization,—intelligent, God-fearing, liberty-loving, self-governed, and bound together in one tender and beautiful brotherhood; our broad, unoccupied acres South and West furnishing homes to millions of exiles and strangers and fellow-countrymen; our soldiers resuming the peaceful pursuits of industry, and infiltrating with their ideas and influence the territories whose rebellion they have subdued; our mighty streams lined with thriving cities, and the seas dotted all over with our white-winged fleets of commerce, and our example giving cheer and hope to each struggling nationality on the globe, and, in the end, sending a purer current through all the avenues of its rejuvenated life!

Men and brethren, has not our Valley of Achor become a door of hope? Have we not something to be thankful for? Is it not meet that *we*, like Israel, at length, in *their* valley of trouble, "Sing here, as in the days of our youth, as in the day that we came up out of Egypt?"

I am mindful of what has been endured. All have been incommoded. Some have suffered, sorely suffered. Multitudes have fallen, and multitudes are sick or maimed for life. Ay, this is the sad part of it! *Graves* have been opened in this valley. There are vacant chairs by festive boards to-day. And some of you have come up here with hearts pained with apprehension, or breaking with grief from the death of father, or son, or husband, or brother, or lover.

But I trust that even you will be able to kiss the rod, and say:

> "If, for the age to come, this hour
> Of trial hath vicarious power,
> And, blest by Thee, our present pain
> Be Liberty's eternal gain,
> *Thy will be done:*"

and that we all will lose sight of our sorrows in our more numerous blessings.

Let, then, thanksgiving ascend from every heart and every tongue. Let us bless God that he has afflicted us. Let us bless him for the war, if only by it these ends could be gained. Let us bless him that it did not come to an earlier and disastrous close, but that it lasts so long as the sin-canker remains. Let us bless him for so good a PRESIDENT: whose love of liberty, coupled with a sacred regard for his oath; whose singleness of purpose and sterling integrity; whose quick common sense and wonderful foresight; whose carefulness to advance and tenacity in holding a position once taken; and whose skill in steering clear of factions and uniting all classes in his support, bid fair to place the name of ABRAHAM LINCOLN beside that of GEORGE WASHINGTON. Let us bless God for the able civil and military leaders the crisis has produced. Let us bless him for our brave soldiers, so prompt to hurl themselves into the deadly breach. Let us bless him for peace with foreign powers, and the tokens of its continuance. Let us bless him for our recent brilliant victories in the field, and the not less important victories in freedom's behalf at the ballot-box.

And, passing now from these causes of gladness, I call on you to praise him for the mercies of the year, of which we have all been recipients. Praise him for the bounties of his providence, from which all have been fed. Praise him for the health vouchsafed so generally to the people. Praise him for the success of all branches of industry, so that none have been compelled to be idle. Praise him for his beautiful light, and the rain-drops, and the pure air of heaven. Praise him for your quiet homes, and your social and religious enjoyments. Praise him for his Bible, and his Sabbath, and his DEAR SON, OUR SAVIOUR! Praise him that he forgiveth our sins and blotteth out all our iniquities. Praise him for *all* present good, and for all the precious hopes of good to come. Yea, praise him! PRAISE him, for HE IS good, and his mercy endureth forever! And let us all now stand up together and unite in our doxology of praise:

"Praise God from whom all blessings flow;
Praise him all creatures here below;
Praise him above, ye heavenly host;
Praise Father, Son, and Holy Ghost."

www.ingramcontent.com/pod-product-compliance
Lightning Source LLC
LaVergne TN
LVHW011142110826
845150LV00008B/2469

*9781418195199*